MAD LIBS®

HISTORY OF THE WORLD
MAD LIBS

concept created by Roger Price & Leonard Stern

MAD LIBS
An Imprint of Penguin Random House LLC, New York

Mad Libs format and text copyright © 2015 by Penguin Random House LLC. All rights reserved.

Concept created by Roger Price & Leonard Stern

Photo credit: cover, page 1: (The Sphinx and Pyramid) © Getty Images, photo by Niko Guido

Published by Mad Libs,
an imprint of Penguin Random House LLC, New York.
Printed in the USA.

Visit us online at www.penguinrandomhouse.com.

ISBN 9780843180756
13

MAD LIBS

INSTRUCTIONS

MAD LIBS® is a game for people who don't like games!
It can be played by one, two, three, four, or forty.

● RIDICULOUSLY SIMPLE DIRECTIONS

In this tablet you will find stories containing blank spaces where words
are left out. One player, the READER, selects one of these stories. The
READER does not tell anyone what the story is about. Instead, he/she asks
the other players, the WRITERS, to give him/her words. These words are
used to fill in the blank spaces in the story.

● TO PLAY

The READER asks each WRITER in turn to call out a word—an adjective or
a noun or whatever the space calls for—and uses them to fill in the blank
spaces in the story. The result is a MAD LIBS® game.

When the READER then reads the completed MAD LIBS® game to the other
players, they will discover that they have written a story that is fantastic,
screamingly funny, shocking, silly, crazy, or just plain dumb—depending
upon which words each WRITER called out.

● EXAMPLE (*Before* and *After*)

" _____ !" he said _____
       EXCLAMATION   ADVERB

as he jumped into his convertible _____ and
                                                    NOUN

drove off with his _____ wife.
                              ADJECTIVE

" _____*Ouch*_____ !" he said _____*stupidly*_____
       EXCLAMATION   ADVERB

as he jumped into his convertible _____*cat*_____ and
                                                    NOUN

drove off with his _____*brave*_____ wife.
                              ADJECTIVE

In case you have forgotten what adjectives, adverbs, nouns, and verbs are, here is a quick review:

An ADJECTIVE describes something or somebody. *Lumpy, soft, ugly, messy,* and *short* are adjectives.

An ADVERB tells how something is done. It modifies a verb and usually ends in "ly." *Modestly, stupidly, greedily,* and *carefully* are adverbs.

A NOUN is the name of a person, place, or thing. *Sidewalk, umbrella, bridle, bathtub,* and *nose* are nouns.

A VERB is an action word. *Run, pitch, jump,* and *swim* are verbs. Put the verbs in past tense if the directions say PAST TENSE. *Ran, pitched, jumped,* and *swam* are verbs in the past tense.

When we ask for A PLACE, we mean any sort of place: a country or city (*Spain, Cleveland*) or a room (*bathroom, kitchen*).

An EXCLAMATION or SILLY WORD is any sort of funny sound, gasp, grunt, or outcry, like *Wow!, Ouch!, Whomp!, Ick!,* and *Gadzooks!*

When we ask for specific words, like a NUMBER, a COLOR, an ANIMAL, or a PART OF THE BODY, we mean a word that is one of those things, like *seven, blue, horse,* or *head.*

When we ask for a PLURAL, it means more than one. For example, *cat* pluralized is *cats.*

MAD LIBS® is fun to play with friends, but you can also play it by yourself! To begin with, DO NOT look at the story on the page below. Fill in the blanks on this page with the words called for. Then, using the words you have selected, fill in the blank spaces in the story.

Now you've created your own hilarious MAD LIBS® game!

LIGHT MY FIRE

PART OF THE BODY (PLURAL) _____

ADJECTIVE _____

ADJECTIVE _____

ADJECTIVE _____

A PLACE _____

ANIMAL _____

PART OF THE BODY _____

NOUN _____

ADJECTIVE _____

ADVERB _____

EXCLAMATION _____

ADJECTIVE _____

PERSON IN ROOM _____

NOUN _____

MAD LIBS®

LIGHT MY FIRE

At one time man walked on four _____, spoke
PART OF THE BODY (PLURAL)

in _____ grunts, and did not know how to make a/an
ADJECTIVE

_____ fire. Here is the story of the day that changed mankind
ADJECTIVE

forever (translated from the _____ cave-speak):
ADJECTIVE

Caveman #1: It's colder than (the) _____ in this cave. Even my
A PLACE

warmest _____ fur won't keep my _____ from shivering.
ANIMAL PART OF THE BODY

Caveman #2: If only there was a way to make the cold _____
NOUN

warmer.

Caveman #1: I'm bored. I think I'll play with these _____
ADJECTIVE

sticks of wood.

Caveman #2: Why don't you rub them _____ together and
ADVERB

see what happens?

Caveman #1: _____! There's smoke coming off these
EXCLAMATION

_____ sticks!
ADJECTIVE

Caveman #2: Ouch! It's hot! In the name of _____—we
PERSON IN ROOM

made heat!

Caveman #1: We shall call this magical flaming _____ *fire*.
NOUN

MAD LIBS® is fun to play with friends, but you can also play it by yourself! To begin with, DO NOT look at the story on the page below. Fill in the blanks on this page with the words called for. Then, using the words you have selected, fill in the blank spaces in the story.

Now you've created your own hilarious MAD LIBS® game!

EUREKA!

PLURAL NOUN _____

OCCUPATION (PLURAL) _____

NOUN _____

PLURAL NOUN _____

PLURAL NOUN _____

NOUN _____

NOUN _____

PLURAL NOUN _____

PLURAL NOUN _____

ADJECTIVE _____

NOUN _____

NOUN _____

NOUN _____

MAD LIBS

EUREKA!

Throughout history, inventors have been responsible for everyday

things like computers, cars, and _____. These are some
PLURAL NOUN

of the most famous _____ in history:
OCCUPATION (PLURAL)

Benjamin Franklin was not only a founding _____ of the
NOUN

United States, he also invented many things, including bifocal glasses,

which allow people to see _____ near and far. He also
PLURAL NOUN

invented the lightning rod, which protects _____ from
PLURAL NOUN

electric bolts of _____.
NOUN

Johannes Gutenberg was a German _____ who invented the
NOUN

printing press, a machine that could print words and _____
PLURAL NOUN

to make books, newspapers, and _____.
PLURAL NOUN

Thomas Edison was a/an _____ inventor perhaps best
ADJECTIVE

known for making a lightbulb that the average _____
NOUN

could use. He also invented the phonograph, which was the first

_____ to be able to record the human _____ and
NOUN   NOUN

then play it back.

MAD LIBS® is fun to play with friends, but you can also play it by yourself! To begin with, DO NOT look at the story on the page below. Fill in the blanks on this page with the words called for. Then, using the words you have selected, fill in the blank spaces in the story.

Now you've created your own hilarious MAD LIBS® game!

NEWSFLASH!: WORLD NOT FLAT

ADJECTIVE _____

ADJECTIVE _____

NOUN _____

TYPE OF FOOD _____

PLURAL NOUN _____

VERB (PAST TENSE) _____

NOUN _____

PLURAL NOUN _____

ADJECTIVE _____

SILLY WORD _____

ADJECTIVE _____

PERSON IN ROOM (FEMALE) _____

ADJECTIVE _____

MAD LIBS
NEWSFLASH!:
WORLD NOT FLAT

In _____ news for explorers everywhere, it has recently been
    ADJECTIVE

discovered that the Earth is round. That's right: Earth is shaped like a/an

_____ ball! For as long as any _____ can remember, it
  ADJECTIVE   NOUN

has been widely believed that the Earth is as flat as a/an _____ .
                         TYPE OF FOOD

_____ believed that if you _____ too
  PLURAL NOUN   VERB (PAST TENSE)

far, you would fall off the edge of the _____ . Now, some
                  NOUN

_____ are trying to prove that the _____ Earth
  PLURAL NOUN   ADJECTIVE

rotates around the sun, though most people think this is a bunch of

_____! We will keep you updated as this _____ story
  SILLY WORD   ADJECTIVE

develops. In the meantime, back to you, _____ , with
               PERSON IN ROOM (FEMALE)

the day's _____ stories.
    ADJECTIVE

MAD LIBS® is fun to play with friends, but you can also play it by yourself! To begin with, DO NOT look at the story on the page below. Fill in the blanks on this page with the words called for. Then, using the words you have selected, fill in the blank spaces in the story.

Now you've created your own hilarious MAD LIBS® game!

CAT FANCY

ADJECTIVE _____

PLURAL NOUN _____

ADJECTIVE _____

PLURAL NOUN _____

ADJECTIVE _____

ADJECTIVE _____

PLURAL NOUN _____

ADJECTIVE _____

NOUN _____

ADVERB _____

PART OF THE BODY (PLURAL) _____

NOUN _____

PLURAL NOUN _____

ADJECTIVE _____

CAT FANCY

You might say the ancient Egyptians were _____ cat people.
                                         ADJECTIVE

After all, they built an entire religion around worshipping their feline

_____! Cats were well-liked by Egyptians for their ability
PLURAL NOUN

to kill _____ vermin like rodents and wild _____.
        ADJECTIVE   _PLURAL NOUN_

Cats were thought to be graceful and _____ creatures. Some
                                      ADJECTIVE

_____ cats were mummified and buried in _____
ADJECTIVE   _PLURAL NOUN_

along with their _____ owners. Harming a cat was a crime
                 ADJECTIVE

punishable by _____. And when a cat died, its family would
              NOUN

mourn _____, shaving their _____ as
      ADVERB   _PART OF THE BODY (PLURAL)_

a symbol of their _____. So maybe it's a little funny that
                  NOUN

ancient _____ worshipped cats. But, then again, so does
        PLURAL NOUN

the _____ Internet!
    ADJECTIVE

MAD LIBS® is fun to play with friends, but you can also play it by yourself! To begin with, DO NOT look at the story on the page below. Fill in the blanks on this page with the words called for. Then, using the words you have selected, fill in the blank spaces in the story.

Now you've created your own hilarious MAD LIBS® game!

THE CODE
OF THE SAMURAI

ADJECTIVE _____

ADJECTIVE _____

PLURAL NOUN _____

ADJECTIVE _____

PLURAL NOUN _____

VERB _____

PLURAL NOUN _____

PLURAL NOUN _____

NOUN _____

PLURAL NOUN _____

VERB _____

PLURAL NOUN _____

NOUN _____

MAD LIBS
THE CODE
OF THE SAMURAI

Samurai were ancient, _____ Japanese warriors who followed
                          ADJECTIVE

a/an _____ code of virtue, which contained these eight
         ADJECTIVE

_____:
   PLURAL NOUN

1. Samurai believed **justice** was the most _____ virtue.
                                                  ADJECTIVE

2. They always showed **courage** in the face of _____.
                                                      PLURAL NOUN

3. Samurai may have had the power to _____, but they also
                                          VERB

   needed to show **mercy** toward all _____.
                                          PLURAL NOUN

4. It was important to be **polite** and considerate of other people's

   _____.
      PLURAL NOUN

5. Samurai also thought **honesty** was the best _____.
                                                     NOUN

6. _____ were not an option for the Samurai, who tried
      PLURAL NOUN

   to _____ with **honor**.
         VERB

7. Samurai were **loyal** to their fellow _____.
                                              PLURAL NOUN

8. And, finally, they had to show **character** and that they knew the

   difference between right and _____.
                                   NOUN

MAD LIBS® is fun to play with friends, but you can also play it by yourself! To begin with, DO NOT look at the story on the page below. Fill in the blanks on this page with the words called for. Then, using the words you have selected, fill in the blank spaces in the story.

Now you've created your own hilarious MAD LIBS® game!

GOD SAVE THE QUEEN

PERSON IN ROOM (MALE) _____

PERSON IN ROOM (FEMALE) _____

NUMBER _____

NOUN _____

VERB ENDING IN "ING" _____

ADJECTIVE _____

FIRST NAME (MALE) _____

ADJECTIVE _____

PERSON IN ROOM _____

A PLACE _____

A PLACE _____

PLURAL NOUN _____

ADJECTIVE _____

PLURAL NOUN _____

NOUN _____

PART OF THE BODY _____

MAD LIBS

GOD SAVE THE QUEEN

Elizabeth I of England was the daughter of King _____

PERSON IN ROOM (MALE)

VIII and his wife _____. At age _____, she was

PERSON IN ROOM (FEMALE)   NUMBER

crowned _____ of England in a royal _____

NOUN   VERB ENDING IN "ING"

ceremony. During her reign, England was a very _____

ADJECTIVE

place to live. Famous writer _____ Shakespeare wrote

FIRST NAME (MALE)

many _____ plays, and explorer _____ discovered

ADJECTIVE   PERSON IN ROOM

(the) _____. In a war against (the) _____, Queen

A PLACE   A PLACE

Elizabeth I led her army of _____ to a/an _____

PLURAL NOUN   ADJECTIVE

victory. Today, many _____ consider Queen Elizabeth the

PLURAL NOUN

most famous _____ in English history. Some even say she

NOUN

ruled England with an iron _____!

PART OF THE BODY

MAD LIBS® is fun to play with friends, but you can also play it by yourself! To begin with, DO NOT look at the story on the page below. Fill in the blanks on this page with the words called for. Then, using the words you have selected, fill in the blank spaces in the story.

Now you've created your own hilarious MAD LIBS® game!

WHAT A
*WONDER*FUL WORLD

NOUN _____

ADJECTIVE _____

NOUN _____

ADJECTIVE _____

PERSON IN ROOM (FEMALE) _____

NOUN _____

CELEBRITY (FEMALE) _____

COLOR _____

CELEBRITY (MALE) _____

PERSON IN ROOM _____

PERSON IN ROOM _____

A PLACE _____

CELEBRITY (MALE) _____

A PLACE _____

NOUN _____

MAD LIBS
WHAT A
WONDERFUL WORLD

These are considered the Seven Wonders of the Ancient _____:

NOUN

1. **The Giza Necropolis** is a site in Egypt where you can see the Great

   Pyramids and the _____ Sphinx.

ADJECTIVE

2. **The Hanging Gardens** were in the ancient _____ of

NOUN

   Babylon and were built as a gift from Nebuchadnezzar II to his

   _____ wife, _____.

ADJECTIVE   PERSON IN ROOM (FEMALE)

3. **The Temple of Artemis at Ephesus** was a Greek _____

NOUN

   dedicated to the goddess _____.

CELEBRITY (FEMALE)

4. **The Statue of Zeus at Olympia** was a forty-three-foot ivory and

   _____ statue of _____.

COLOR   CELEBRITY (MALE)

5. **The Mausoleum at Halicarnassus** was a tomb built by

   _____ and _____ of (the) _____.

PERSON IN ROOM   PERSON IN ROOM   A PLACE

6. **The Colossus of Rhodes** was a statue of Greek god _____,

CELEBRITY (MALE)

   built to commemorate victory over (the) _____.

A PLACE

7. **The Lighthouse of Alexandria** was at one time the tallest

   _____ on Earth.

NOUN

MAD LIBS® is fun to play with friends, but you can also play it by yourself! To begin with, DO NOT look at the story on the page below. Fill in the blanks on this page with the words called for. Then, using the words you have selected, fill in the blank spaces in the story.

Now you've created your own hilarious MAD LIBS® game!

FAMOUS FIRSTS

PERSON IN ROOM _____

NOUN _____

PERSON IN ROOM _____

NOUN _____

NOUN _____

PERSON IN ROOM _____

PERSON IN ROOM _____

PLURAL NOUN _____

PERSON IN ROOM _____

PART OF THE BODY _____

A PLACE _____

PERSON IN ROOM _____

VERB _____

PERSON IN ROOM _____

ANIMAL _____

MAD LIBS

FAMOUS FIRSTS

- In 1901, _____ became the first person to go over
  PERSON IN ROOM

  Niagara Falls in a/an _____ and survive.
  NOUN

- In 1933, _____ became the first _____ to fly an
  PERSON IN ROOM   NOUN

  airplane around the _____.
  NOUN

- In 1953, _____ and _____ became the first
  PERSON IN ROOM   PERSON IN ROOM

  _____ to climb to the top of Mount Everest.
  PLURAL NOUN

- In 1963, _____ became the first person to receive a/an
  PERSON IN ROOM

  _____ transplant in (the) _____, South Africa.
  PART OF THE BODY   A PLACE

- In 1969, _____ became the first person to _____
  PERSON IN ROOM   VERB

  on the moon.

- In 1996, in Scotland, _____ became the world's first clone
  PERSON IN ROOM

  of a/an _____.
  ANIMAL

MAD LIBS® is fun to play with friends, but you can also play it by yourself! To begin with, DO NOT look at the story on the page below. Fill in the blanks on this page with the words called for. Then, using the words you have selected, fill in the blank spaces in the story.

Now you've created your own hilarious MAD LIBS® game!

LAND, HO!

PLURAL NOUN _____

PLURAL NOUN _____

ADJECTIVE _____

NOUN _____

VERB (PAST TENSE) _____

ADJECTIVE _____

NOUN _____

NOUN _____

NOUN _____

NOUN _____

PLURAL NOUN _____

NOUN _____

PERSON IN ROOM (FEMALE) _____

PLURAL NOUN _____

PART OF THE BODY _____

PLURAL NOUN _____

MAD LIBS®
LAND, HO!

Throughout history, _____ with a sense of adventure have
                       PLURAL NOUN

traveled the world in search of new lands and _____. Here
                                               PLURAL NOUN

are a few of the most _____ explorers:
                       ADJECTIVE

Leif Ericson was a famous Viking _____ who
                                      NOUN

_____ to the Americas five hundred years before
VERB (PAST TENSE)

_____ Christopher Columbus.
ADJECTIVE

Ferdinand Magellan, a Portuguese _____, became the
                                      NOUN

first _____ to cross the Pacific Ocean while he tried to
      NOUN

discover a route to the _____ Islands.
                        NOUN

Marco Polo traveled in a/an _____ from Italy to China
                                 NOUN

and helped many Western _____ learn about the
                         PLURAL NOUN

Eastern _____ .
        NOUN

Lewis and Clark, led by _____, were the
                            PERSON IN ROOM (FEMALE)

first _____ to travel by _____ across the
      PLURAL NOUN   PART OF THE BODY

continental United _____ .
                   PLURAL NOUN

MAD LIBS® is fun to play with friends, but you can also play it by yourself! To begin with, DO NOT look at the story on the page below. Fill in the blanks on this page with the words called for. Then, using the words you have selected, fill in the blank spaces in the story.

Now you've created your own hilarious MAD LIBS® game!

WALK LIKE AN EGYPTIAN

ADJECTIVE _____

NOUN _____

ADJECTIVE _____

ADJECTIVE _____

PLURAL NOUN _____

ADJECTIVE _____

PLURAL NOUN _____

ADVERB _____

NOUN _____

NOUN _____

VERB (PAST TENSE) _____

ADJECTIVE _____

OCCUPATION _____

NOUN _____

CELEBRITY (FEMALE) _____

MAD☺LIBS®

WALK LIKE AN EGYPTIAN

Cleopatra was a/an _____ Egyptian pharaoh. Well-
ADJECTIVE
educated and clever as a/an _____, Cleopatra spoke many
NOUN
_____ languages. She was also known for being particularly
ADJECTIVE
_____ . When she was eighteen, Cleopatra took the throne,
ADJECTIVE
though she was chased out by a bunch of unruly _____.
PLURAL NOUN
In response, Cleopatra put together an army of _____
ADJECTIVE
_____ , marched _____ back into Egypt, and took
PLURAL NOUN   ADVERB
back the _____ for herself. Cleopatra fell in love with the Roman
NOUN
_____ , Julius Caesar. After Caesar _____,
NOUN   VERB (PAST TENSE)
Cleopatra fell in love with another _____ Roman, Mark
ADJECTIVE
Antony. Cleopatra was the most famous and powerful _____
OCCUPATION
to rule a/an _____ . She was even played by the legendary
NOUN
actress _____ in a movie about her life!
CELEBRITY (FEMALE)

MAD LIBS® is fun to play with friends, but you can also play it by yourself! To begin with, DO NOT look at the story on the page below. Fill in the blanks on this page with the words called for. Then, using the words you have selected, fill in the blank spaces in the story.

Now you've created your own hilarious MAD LIBS® game!

CROOKS DOWN UNDER

NOUN _____

ADJECTIVE _____

PLURAL NOUN _____

ADJECTIVE _____

PERSON IN ROOM _____

ADJECTIVE _____

NUMBER _____

PLURAL NOUN _____

ADJECTIVE _____

VERB _____

PLURAL NOUN _____

PERSON IN ROOM (FEMALE) _____

ANIMAL _____

NUMBER _____

PART OF THE BODY _____

MAD LIBS

CROOKS DOWN UNDER

Australia—known as the _____ Down Under—has a/an
NOUN

_____ criminal past. In the late 1700s, Britain's prisons were
ADJECTIVE

overrun with _____, so they began transporting their
PLURAL NOUN

_____ prisoners to Australia. Captain _____ was in
ADJECTIVE   PERSON IN ROOM

charge of setting up the first _____ colony for prisoners. Over
ADJECTIVE

_____ years, fifty-five thousand criminal _____
NUMBER   PLURAL NOUN

came from England to live there! With _____ behavior, these
ADJECTIVE

prisoners could _____ their way to freedom and gain work as
VERB

butchers, farmers, and professional _____. One resident
PLURAL NOUN

in the colony was a thirteen-year-old named _____,
PERSON IN ROOM (FEMALE)

who had come to the colony for stealing a/an _____. She
ANIMAL

eventually became one of Australia's first businesswomen, and today,

Australia's _____-dollar bill features her _____!
NUMBER   PART OF THE BODY

MAD LIBS® is fun to play with friends, but you can also play it by yourself! To begin with, DO NOT look at the story on the page below. Fill in the blanks on this page with the words called for. Then, using the words you have selected, fill in the blank spaces in the story.

Now you've created your own hilarious MAD LIBS® game!

WHEREFORE ART THOU SHAKESPEARE?

NOUN _____

PERSON IN ROOM (FEMALE) _____

NOUN _____

ADJECTIVE _____

ADJECTIVE _____

NOUN _____

ADJECTIVE _____

PLURAL NOUN _____

NOUN _____

NOUN _____

NOUN _____

PLURAL NOUN _____

PART OF THE BODY (PLURAL) _____

NOUN _____

MAD☻LIBS®
WHEREFORE ART THOU SHAKESPEARE?

William Shakespeare is the most famous writer in the history of

the _____. He wrote many plays, including *Romeo and*
       NOUN

_____ and *A Midsummer Night's* _____. He
PERSON IN ROOM (FEMALE)   NOUN

also wrote many _____ poems. Here is a selection from one
              ADJECTIVE

of his most _____ sonnets:
        ADJECTIVE

       Shall I compare thee to a summer's _____?
                                    NOUN

      Thou art more lovely and more _____.
                              ADJECTIVE

    Rough winds do shake the darling _____ of May,
                              PLURAL NOUN

And summer's _____ hath all too short a/an _____ . . .
            NOUN   NOUN

      But thy eternal _____ shall not fade . . .
                        NOUN

So long as _____ can breathe, or _____
           PLURAL NOUN   PART OF THE BODY (PLURAL)

              can see,

    So long lives this, and this gives _____ to thee.
                                   NOUN

MAD LIBS® is fun to play with friends, but you can also play it by yourself! To begin with, DO NOT look at the story on the page below. Fill in the blanks on this page with the words called for. Then, using the words you have selected, fill in the blank spaces in the story.

Now you've created your own hilarious MAD LIBS® game!

WANTED:
FOUNTAIN OF YOUTH

ADJECTIVE _____

VERB ENDING IN "S" _____

ANIMAL _____

PART OF THE BODY _____

ADJECTIVE _____

PLURAL NOUN _____

A PLACE _____

ADJECTIVE _____

SILLY WORD _____

NOUN _____

PLURAL NOUN _____

NOUN _____

MAD LIBS
WANTED:
FOUNTAIN OF YOUTH

Spanish explorer Ponce de Leon seeks a/an _____ Fountain of
                                          ADJECTIVE
Youth. Anyone who drinks or _____ in its waters will
                            VERB ENDING IN "S"
have eternal youth. It can also cure illnesses from _____ pox to
                                                    ANIMAL
the _____ flu. It has been rumored for many _____
    PART OF THE BODY   ADJECTIVE
years that the Fountain of Youth exists. Some _____
                                              PLURAL NOUN
believe it is either in the New World or (the) _____. If you
                                               A PLACE
find this _____ fountain, please contact Ponce de Leon at
          ADJECTIVE
555-_____ or poncedeleon@_____-mail.com. You
     SILLY WORD   NOUN
will be rewarded with gold and _____, as well as eternal
                               PLURAL NOUN
_____.
    NOUN

MAD LIBS® is fun to play with friends, but you can also play it by yourself! To begin with, DO NOT look at the story on the page below. Fill in the blanks on this page with the words called for. Then, using the words you have selected, fill in the blank spaces in the story.

Now you've created your own hilarious MAD LIBS® game!

O.M.O. (OH MY ODIN)

PLURAL NOUN _____

A PLACE _____

ADJECTIVE _____

A PLACE _____

PLURAL NOUN _____

VERB _____

ADJECTIVE _____

COLOR _____

SAME COLOR _____

ADJECTIVE _____

ADJECTIVE _____

PLURAL NOUN _____

PLURAL NOUN _____

PLURAL NOUN _____

PLURAL NOUN _____

NOUN _____

MAD LIBS

O.M.O. (OH MY ODIN)

Vikings were seafaring _____ from Scandinavia, which
PLURAL NOUN

includes modern-day countries like Denmark, Norway, and (the)

_____. Vikings traveled in their _____ boats
A PLACE   ADJECTIVE

from Europe to Russia and then to (the) _____, raiding
A PLACE

_____ and establishing villages to _____ in. The
PLURAL NOUN   VERB

Vikings were known to be _____ fighters. One famous Viking
ADJECTIVE

warrior was Erik the _____, who was nicknamed this because
COLOR

of his flowing _____ beard. There were also _____
SAME COLOR   ADJECTIVE

Viking female warriors who wore _____ shields when fighting
ADJECTIVE

_____. The Vikings even had their own gods and goddesses,
PLURAL NOUN

like Odin, who was thought to be the ruler of all _____,
PLURAL NOUN

and who also represented war, battle, and _____. The
PLURAL NOUN

Vikings were a serious bunch of _____—you sure didn't
PLURAL NOUN

want to get on their bad _____!
NOUN

MAD LIBS® is fun to play with friends, but you can also play it by yourself! To begin with, DO NOT look at the story on the page below. Fill in the blanks on this page with the words called for. Then, using the words you have selected, fill in the blank spaces in the story.

Now you've created your own hilarious MAD LIBS® game!

PEACE, LOVE, AND

_____
PLURAL NOUN

PLURAL NOUN _____

ADJECTIVE _____

PLURAL NOUN _____

NOUN _____

PLURAL NOUN _____

A PLACE _____

VERB ENDING IN "ING" _____

PLURAL NOUN _____

NOUN _____

NOUN _____

A PLACE _____

ADJECTIVE _____

A PLACE _____

PLURAL NOUN _____

PLURAL NOUN _____

MAD LIBS®
PEACE, LOVE, AND
_____
PLURAL NOUN

Since the beginning of time, _____ have fought with one
PLURAL NOUN

another for many _____ reasons. But these brave people
ADJECTIVE

devoted their lives to helping their fellow _____:
PLURAL NOUN

Gandhi led India to freedom from the British _____, who
NOUN

had taken it over. He inspired people all over the world to be peaceful

_____.
PLURAL NOUN

Martin Luther King Jr. led the Civil Rights Movement in (the)

_____, helping gain equal rights for African Americans by
A PLACE

_____ peacefully.
VERB ENDING IN "ING"

Nelson Mandela helped end racist _____ in South Africa.
PLURAL NOUN

For his hard work, he won the Nobel Peace _____ and the US
NOUN

Presidential _____ of Freedom.
NOUN

Mother Teresa was a nun from (the) _____ who devoted her life
A PLACE

to helping sick and _____ people all over (the) _____.
ADJECTIVE _A PLACE_

Clara Barton was a nurse who helped found the American Red

Cross, which educates _____ and gives assistance to
PLURAL NOUN

_____ in need.
PLURAL NOUN

MAD LIBS® is fun to play with friends, but you can also play it by yourself! To begin with, DO NOT look at the story on the page below. Fill in the blanks on this page with the words called for. Then, using the words you have selected, fill in the blank spaces in the story.

Now you've created your own hilarious MAD LIBS® game!

DID I DO THAT?

PLURAL NOUN _____

PLURAL NOUN _____

PERSON IN ROOM _____

NOUN _____

PLURAL NOUN _____

VERB _____

NOUN _____

PERSON IN ROOM (MALE) _____

VERB _____

VERB _____

ADJECTIVE _____

A PLACE _____

ADJECTIVE _____

PERSON IN ROOM _____

NOUN _____

ADJECTIVE _____

MAD☺LIBS®

DID I DO THAT?

Oops! We should thank our lucky _____ for these
___PLURAL NOUN___
_____ that were invented by accident!
PLURAL NOUN

The microwave: In 1945, _____ was experimenting
___PERSON IN ROOM___
with a/an _____ when he discovered it could melt
___NOUN___
_____ and make popcorn _____. He then
___PLURAL NOUN___   ___VERB___
built the first microwave _____.
___NOUN___

The Slinky: In 1943, naval engineer _____
___PERSON IN ROOM (MALE)___
attempted to create a spring to help ships _____, when
___VERB___
he got the idea for a toy spring that could _____ down the
___VERB___
stairs all by itself. It became the _____ Slinky!
___ADJECTIVE___

Potato chips: At a restaurant in (the) _____ in
___A PLACE___
1853, a customer complained that his fried potatoes were too
_____. The chef, _____, cut the potatoes as thin
___ADJECTIVE___   ___PERSON IN ROOM___
as possible and fried them to a/an _____, accidentally
___NOUN___
inventing the _____ potato chip!
___ADJECTIVE___

MAD LIBS® is fun to play with friends, but you can also play it by yourself! To begin with, DO NOT look at the story on the page below. Fill in the blanks on this page with the words called for. Then, using the words you have selected, fill in the blank spaces in the story.

Now you've created your own hilarious MAD LIBS® game!

STATE OF WONDER

NOUN _____

PLURAL NOUN _____

ADJECTIVE _____

PLURAL NOUN _____

A PLACE _____

A PLACE _____

ADJECTIVE _____

PLURAL NOUN _____

PLURAL NOUN _____

ADJECTIVE _____

NOUN _____

ADJECTIVE _____

NOUN _____

ADJECTIVE _____

PERSON IN ROOM (MALE) _____

CELEBRITY _____

The Seven Wonders of the Modern _____ were chosen by
NOUN

_____ like me and you!
PLURAL NOUN

1. **The Great Wall of China** is a/an _____ wall made of
ADJECTIVE

stones, bricks, and _____ that stretches all the way
PLURAL NOUN

from (the) _____ to (the) _____.
A PLACE   A PLACE

2. **Petra** is a/an _____ city in Jordan, also known as the
ADJECTIVE

Rose City for its pink-colored _____.
PLURAL NOUN

3. **The Coliseum** is an ancient Roman amphitheater built by

_____.
PLURAL NOUN

4. **Chichen Itza** is a/an _____ city in Mexico built during
ADJECTIVE

the _____ Empire.
NOUN

5. **Machu Picchu** is a/an _____ estate built into a huge
ADJECTIVE

_____ in Peru.
NOUN

6. **Taj Mahal** is a/an _____ mausoleum in India, built by
ADJECTIVE

Emperor _____.
PERSON IN ROOM (MALE)

7. **Christ the Redeemer** in Brazil is a hundred-foot-tall statue of

_____.
CELEBRITY

MAD LIBS® is fun to play with friends, but you can also play it by yourself! To begin with, DO NOT look at the story on the page below. Fill in the blanks on this page with the words called for. Then, using the words you have selected, fill in the blank spaces in the story.

Now you've created your own hilarious MAD LIBS® game!

MONGOLIAN WARRIOR

ADJECTIVE _____

NUMBER _____

ADJECTIVE _____

PLURAL NOUN _____

ADJECTIVE _____

A PLACE _____

PLURAL NOUN _____

ADJECTIVE _____

PLURAL NOUN _____

PLURAL NOUN _____

ADJECTIVE _____

NOUN _____

ADJECTIVE _____

VERB (PAST TENSE) _____

ADJECTIVE _____

MAD LIBS

MONGOLIAN WARRIOR

Genghis Khan was a/an _____ Mongolian leader. Starting
                              ADJECTIVE

at the young age of _____, Genghis Khan began to build
                          NUMBER

a/an _____ army of _____. He wanted to
          ADJECTIVE   PLURAL NOUN

destroy _____ tribes in (the) Northeast _____ so
              ADJECTIVE   A PLACE

he could rule over all the _____ in the land. He and his
                                  PLURAL NOUN

_____ armies marched into _____ all around
     ADJECTIVE   PLURAL NOUN

Asia. They brutally fought and killed many _____ and
                                                    PLURAL NOUN

eventually created the _____ Mongolian Empire, which
                              ADJECTIVE

was the largest _____ in the world. Today, Genghis Khan is
                      NOUN

considered one of the most ruthless and _____ warriors that
                                                ADJECTIVE

ever _____. You wouldn't have wanted to meet him
        VERB (PAST TENSE)

alone in a/an _____ alley!
                    ADJECTIVE

MAD LIBS® is fun to play with friends, but you can also play it by yourself! To begin with, DO NOT look at the story on the page below. Fill in the blanks on this page with the words called for. Then, using the words you have selected, fill in the blank spaces in the story.

Now you've created your own hilarious MAD LIBS® game!

NAPOLEON COMPLEX

OCCUPATION _____

PLURAL NOUN _____

PLURAL NOUN _____

ADJECTIVE _____

NOUN _____

NOUN _____

NOUN _____

ADJECTIVE _____

NOUN _____

PLURAL NOUN _____

PLURAL NOUN _____

ADJECTIVE _____

A PLACE _____

A PLACE _____

PLURAL NOUN _____

VERB (PAST TENSE) _____

ADJECTIVE _____

MAD LIBS

NAPOLEON COMPLEX

Napoleon Bonaparte was the first _____ of France. He made
                                      OCCUPATION

his way to the top during the French Revolution, where regular old

_____ rose up to fight against royal _____.
  PLURAL NOUN   PLURAL NOUN

But Napoleon was known for having a/an _____ temper. He
                                              ADJECTIVE

would fly off the _____ at the drop of a/an _____.
                       NOUN   NOUN

Napoleon was also not a very tall _____. Some say his small
                                       NOUN

size made him feel _____. In order to feel like more of
                        ADJECTIVE

a/an _____, he would act out, invade _____, and
          NOUN   PLURAL NOUN

fight wars with _____! This made him feel _____
                   PLURAL NOUN   ADJECTIVE

and powerful, despite his small size. And, for a while, it worked, and

Napoleon ruled over all of (the) _____. But eventually, at
                                      A PLACE

the Battle of (the) _____, Napoleon was captured by British
                        A PLACE

_____, and he _____. One thing's
  PLURAL NOUN   VERB (PAST TENSE)

for sure: What Napoleon lacked in size, he made up for with his

_____ personality!
  ADJECTIVE

MAD LIBS® is fun to play with friends, but you can also play it by yourself! To begin with, DO NOT look at the story on the page below. Fill in the blanks on this page with the words called for. Then, using the words you have selected, fill in the blank spaces in the story.

Now you've created your own hilarious MAD LIBS® game!

WHEN IN ROME

ADJECTIVE _____

PLURAL NOUN _____

ADJECTIVE _____

ADJECTIVE _____

PLURAL NOUN _____

ADJECTIVE _____

PLURAL NOUN _____

VERB _____

ADJECTIVE _____

PART OF THE BODY (PLURAL) _____

PLURAL NOUN _____

NOUN _____

NOUN _____

NOUN _____

The Roman Empire is one of the most _____ empires in world
                                  ADJECTIVE

history. Two thousand years ago, one in four _____ lived
                                           PLURAL NOUN

under Roman rule. The Roman Empire was led by _____
                                                  ADJECTIVE

emperors—a bunch of powerful men who wore _____ robes
                                             ADJECTIVE

and decided the fate of Rome's many _____. The most
                                        PLURAL NOUN

famous Roman emperor was Caesar Augustus, a/an _____
                                                ADJECTIVE

leader who helped Rome become one of the most powerful

_____ the world had ever seen. The Roman people,
PLURAL NOUN

rich and poor, loved to mingle, gossip, and _____ at the
                                                VERB

_____ Roman baths, a place for bathing and exercising your
ADJECTIVE

_____. Romans also enjoyed watching gladiators
PART OF THE BODY (PLURAL)

fight wild _____ in coliseums and racing chariots around
                 PLURAL NOUN

a/an _____. For about five hundred years, Romans ruled the
              NOUN

_____—which is why the Roman Empire is thought of by
NOUN

some people as the most powerful _____ to ever exist.
                                               NOUN

MAD LIBS® is fun to play with friends, but you can also play it by yourself! To begin with, DO NOT look at the story on the page below. Fill in the blanks on this page with the words called for. Then, using the words you have selected, fill in the blank spaces in the story.

Now you've created your own hilarious MAD LIBS® game!

AN APPLE A DAY

ADJECTIVE _____

ADJECTIVE _____

ADJECTIVE _____

ADJECTIVE _____

PERSON IN ROOM (FEMALE) _____

SILLY WORD _____

A PLACE _____

VERB ENDING IN "ING" _____

NOUN _____

ADVERB _____

NOUN _____

ADJECTIVE _____

NOUN _____

ADJECTIVE _____

VERB _____

Here is the story of how a/an _____ scientist named Sir Isaac
                                    ADJECTIVE

Newton came up with the _____ theory of gravity. One day,
                               ADJECTIVE

a/an _____ Isaac went to visit his _____ mother,
        ADJECTIVE   ADJECTIVE

_____ , at _____ Manor, her country home
PERSON IN ROOM (FEMALE)   SILLY WORD

in (the) _____ . While _____ in the garden,
           A PLACE   VERB ENDING IN "ING"

Isaac saw an apple fall from a/an _____ . *Why does that apple*
                                         NOUN

fall _____ *to the ground?* thought Isaac. *Why doesn't the apple*
            ADVERB

fall sideways, or go upward, toward the _____ *in the sky?* Before
                                                  NOUN

long, Isaac decided that the _____ apple must be drawn to the
                                   ADJECTIVE

Earth's core, right in the middle of the _____ . And thus, Sir
                                                 NOUN

Isaac Newton came up with the _____ concept of gravity—
                                     ADJECTIVE

that whatever goes up must _____ down.
                                  VERB

Download Mad Libs today!

Join the millions of Mad Libs fans creating wacky and wonderful stories on our apps!